Lisa Leslie

SPARKS

9

THE STORY OF THE LOS ANGELES SPARKS

Katie Lou Samuelson

WNBA: A HISTORY OF WOMEN'S HOOPS

THE STORY OF THE

LOS ANGELES SPARKS

JIM WHITING

Brittney Sykes

CREATIVE EDUCATION / CREATIVE PAPERBACKS

Published by Creative Education and Creative Paperbacks
P.O. Box 227, Mankato, Minnesota 56002
Creative Education and Creative Paperbacks are imprints of
The Creative Company
www.thecreativecompany.us

Design and production by Blue Design (www.bluedes.com)
Art direction by Rita Marshall

Photographs by Getty (Leon Bennett, Lisa Blumenfeld, Steph Chambers, Tim
Clayton/Corbis, Kevork Djansezian, Otto Greule Jr., Harry How, Kellie Landis,
MediaNews Group/Pasadena Star-News, Meg Oliphant, Sam Wasson, Rocky
Widner)

Library of Congress Cataloging-in-Publication Data
Names: Whiting, Jim, 1943- author.
Title: The Story of the Los Angeles Sparks / by Jim Whiting.
Description: Mankato, Minnesota : Creative Education and Creative
   Paperbacks, [2024] | Series: Creative Sports. WNBA : A History of
   Women's Hoops. | Includes index. | Audience: Ages 8-12 | Audience:
   Grades 4-6 | Summary: "Middle grade basketball fans are introduced to
   the extraordinary history of WNBA's Los Angeles Sparks with a
   photo-laden narrative of their greatest successes and losses"-- Provided
   by publisher.
Identifiers: LCCN 2022034255 (print) | LCCN 2022034256 (ebook) | ISBN
   9781640267220 (library binding) | ISBN 9781682772782 (paperback) | ISBN
   9781640008731 (pdf)
Subjects: LCSH: Los Angeles Sparks (Basketball team)--History--Juvenile
   literature.
Classification: LCC GV885.52.L68 W55 2024 (print) | LCC GV885.52.L68
   (ebook) | DDC 796.323/640979494--dc23/eng/20220720
LC record available at https://lccn.loc.gov/2022034255
LC ebook record available at https://lccn.loc.gov/2022034256

Printed in China

Kristi Toliver

CONTENTS

LEGENDS OF THE HARDWOOD

Alana Beard

8

A SPARK OF EXCITEMENT

The Minnesota Lynx led the Los Angeles Sparks by one point in the deciding Game 5 of the Women's National Basketball Association (WNBA) championship series in 2016. The Sparks had the ball out of bounds with 23.4 seconds remaining. Forward Candace Parker took the pass and curled around a defender to score on a layup with 19.7 seconds remaining. That gave the Sparks a one-point lead. After a timeout, Minnesota star Maya Moore sank a jump shot to put the Lynx back on top with 15.4 seconds left. Los Angeles didn't have any more timeouts, which would have allowed them to set up a play. Speedy Sparks guard Chelsea Gray rushed downcourt with the ball. She put up a short shot with seven seconds left. It bounced off the rim. A cluster of five players leapt up to try to snag the rebound. Los Angeles forward Nneka Ogwumike came down with it. She put up a shot. It was blocked. The ball came right back to her. Ogwumike quickly put up an off-balance shot. She

Lisa Leslie

WHAT'S IN A NAME?

When the WNBA was formed, each team was closely linked with an National Basketball Association (NBA) team in the same city. The WNBA team names were supposed to be related to their corresponding NBA team. For example, the Phoenix NBA team is the Suns. The WNBA team is named the Mercury. Mercury is the closest planet to the sun. The Los Angeles NBA team was the Lakers. It had been founded in Minnesota, which has thousands of lakes. There aren't many lakes in Southern California! Jerry Buss owned both teams. He was having a hard time finding an appropriate nickname. One day he was on the phone with the league office to discuss the situation. At the same time, one of his assistants was on the phone with her dad. He was a welder. When he worked, sparks flew. He suggested Sparks. He thought the name would "spark" energy, enthusiasm, and electricity on the court. Buss agreed. Los Angeles Sparks, it was!

tumbled to the floor as it dropped into the hoop with 3.1 seconds left. A desperation three-point Minnesota shot from midcourt was way off. The Sparks won 77–76. They were WNBA champions!

T he Sparks generated the same excitement when they hosted the WNBA's first-ever game on June 21, 1997, against the New York Liberty. Billboards trumpeted the arrival of the new team. The parking lot of the Great Western Forum was a massive party, with music, food, and people milling around. Banners showing Sparks players hung outside the arena. One depicted guard Penny Toler. "I was an older player— had already done eight years overseas—and coming back to all this," she said. "I felt like a rock star and hadn't even played a game yet." It didn't take long for Toler to live up to the hype. She scored the league's first points on a jump shot 59 seconds into the game. "Looking back on it, it's an honor I love to have," she said later. "There can only be one first basket." The Liberty went on to win, 67–57. Los Angeles spent most of the season just below the .500 level. A four-game winning streak edged them over .500 at 14–13. But they lost the final game. They finished 14–14 and missed a spot in the playoffs by a single game. Center Lisa Leslie led the team with an average of nearly 16 points a game.

The Sparks lost seven of the first nine games in 1998. They finished 12–18 and were far from playoff contention.

After a 3–4 start in 1999, Los Angeles had a six-game winning streak. Another six-game streak soon followed. They finished 20-12 and qualified for the playoffs. They defeated the Sacramento Monarchs in a single-game first round. They faced

the Houston Comets in the Western Conference finals. The Comets had already won the first two league championships. The Sparks opened with a 75–60 victory in the first game. But they lost the next two in the best-of-three series.

The Sparks won their first four games in 2000. After a pair of losses, they won the next 12 in a row. Soon afterward, they had another 12-game streak. They finished 28–4. It was the most wins in league history to that point. The Sparks easily defeated the Phoenix Mercury in the conference semifinals. Once again they faced the Comets in the conference finals. Houston swept the series.

TAKING TWO TITLES

The Sparks won their first nine games in 2001. After losing the next three, they won 18 in a row. That remains the longest winning streak in WNBA history. Again they finished 28–4. Guards Tamecka Dixon and Mwadi Mabika each averaged more than 12 points per game. They swept the Comets in the conference semifinals. Los Angeles edged Sacramento 74–73 in the first game of the conference finals. Leslie and forward DeLisha Mann both blocked potential game-winning shots in the final seconds. After losing Game 2, Los Angeles cruised to a 93–62 win to take the conference championship. Now they faced the Charlotte Sting for the WNBA title. They won the first game 75–66, then followed that up with an 82–54 victory. It was their first WNBA title!

After an early nine-game winning streak in 2002, the Sparks were 12–1. They maintained the momentum and cruised to a 25–7 mark. One highlight came

Tamecka Dixon

on July 30, when Leslie became the first WNBA player to dunk the ball during a game. It was somewhat spontaneous. Leslie said, "I just turned around, and I was free, and I said, 'Oh my God, I'm going to go for it.'" Los Angeles swept the Seattle Storm and Utah Starzz in the first two rounds of the playoffs. They defeated the Liberty 71–63 in Game 1 of the WNBA Finals. Game 2 was tied at 66 with 13 seconds left. Guard Nikki Teasley took a short inbounds pass at halfcourt. She dribbled slowly down the right side of the court. She stopped and faked a pass. When her defender backed off, she launched a three-point shot with less than three seconds left. It went in! The basket gave the Sparks a 69–66 win and their second WNBA title in a row.

Fans hoped for a "three-peat" in 2003. The season began almost exactly like the previous one, with a nine-game winning streak. It ended with an overall 24–10 record. The Sparks had to go to three games against both the Lynx and

Nikki Teasley

LISA LESLIE
CENTER
HEIGHT: 6-FOOT-5
SPARKS SEASONS: 1997–2009

A STAR RIGHT FROM THE START

Growing up in southern California, Lisa Leslie usually played
basketball with boys to develop her skills. She was a natural left-
hander. She taught herself to shoot right-handed to increase her
scoring opportunities. By the time she started high school, she had
received more than 100 college recruiting letters. She chose the
nearby University of Southern California. Leslie was a three-time
All-American with the Trojans. She averaged nearly 16 points and 10
rebounds per game in her first year with the Sparks. She maintained
similar numbers during her entire WNBA career. She was an eight-
time All-Star and named the league's Most Valuable Player (MVP)
three times. She also won four Olympic gold medals. Leslie is regarded
as one of the best all-time female basketball players.

LOS ANGELES SPARKS

Tamecka Dixon

TAMECKA DIXON

GUARD

HEIGHT: 5-FOOT-9

SPARKS SEASONS:

1997-2005

LEADING THE WAY

When she was growing up, Dixon's dream was to be the first girl in the NBA.
While that never happened, Dixon took advantage of the origin of the WNBA
to realize a different version. She graduated from the University of Kansas as
a Second Team All-American in 1997, the year the WNBA began. She was the
third college player to be drafted. She took full advantage of the opportunity.
Dixon averaged more than 10 points a game in her Sparks career. She played in
three All-Star Games. In 2001, she was named to the All-WNBA Second Team.
She never lost sight of her youthful dream. "I felt like with the platform that
I was given, I had a responsibility to show to young girls and young boys that
anything is possible if they put the hard work in," she said.

Monarchs in the first two rounds of the playoffs. Now they faced the Detroit Shock in the WNBA Finals. Los Angeles won Game 1, 75–63. Detroit had a 19-point lead in Game 2, but the Sparks came back. They led by four points with a minute and a half left. Detroit answered with a three-point shot. Deanna Nolan of the Shock was fouled with 12 seconds left. She sank both free throws. Los Angeles couldn't get a shot off in the final moments. Detroit won 62–61.The Sparks had a 73–70 lead late in Game 3 but went scoreless for three minutes. The Shock won 83-78. That ended the chance for three titles in a row.

The 2004 season didn't start as spectacularly as the previous ones. But mid-season winning streaks of six games led to a 25–9 season. It was the sixth year in a row that Los Angeles had at least 20 victories. The Sparks lost two of three games to the Monarchs in the conference semifinals to end their season.

Los Angeles fell off the 20-win pace in 2005. Their longest winning streak was just four games. They finished 17–17. The Monarchs swept them in the conference semifinals.

Highlighted by an early eight-game winning streak and a six-game streak shortly afterward, the Sparks soared to another 25–9 mark in 2006. They defeated the Storm in three games in the conference semifinals. Sacramento knocked them out of the playoffs for the third straight year in the next round.

LEAN YEARS

L isa Leslie missed the entire 2007 season. Los Angeles started 5–2. That proved to be half their win total that season. They went 5–22 the rest of the way and ended with a 10–24 mark. It was the worst record in the league that year. It was also the worst record in team history.

Leslie returned in 2008. In addition, the team took University of Tennessee star Candace Parker with the top overall pick in the 2008 WNBA Draft. Parker had a sensational rookie season. She became the only woman to be named WNBA Rookie of the Year *and* Most Valuable Player in the same season. Wilt Chamberlain and Wes Unseld of the NBA are the only other players to receive both honors. Leslie and Parker helped propel Los Angeles to a 20–14 mark. They defeated Seattle, 2 games to 1, in the conference semifinals. They defeated San Antonio in Game 1 of the conference finals. But they lost Game 2 by a single point on a last-second shot. The Silver Stars won a tight Game 3 to close out the series.

Both Leslie and Parker missed the start of the 2009 season. The Sparks were just 8–14 when they returned. The team went 10–2 the rest of the way to finish 18-16. They took two of three from the Storm in the conference semifinals. But they lost two of three to the Mercury in the conference finals.

Leslie retired after the 2009 season. The Sparks lost six of their first seven games in 2010. Parker had a season-ending shoulder injury soon afterward. Los

Candace Parker

SPARKS

3

boost
mobile

KRISTI TOLIVER
GUARD
HEIGHT: 5-FOOT-7
SPARKS SEASONS:
2010–16, 2020–22

LOOKING TO HER FUTURE

The Chicago Sky made Kristi Toliver the third overall pick in the 2009 WNBA Draft. They traded her to Los Angeles the following season. Toliver became a full-time starter in 2012. She was named to the All-WNBA Second Team that season and became an All-Star in 2013. Toliver scored a franchise-record 43 points in a game in 2015. She left the team after helping guide it to the 2016 WNBA title. Toliver returned to Los Angeles in 2020. But she sat out the season due to COVID-19. She averaged more than nine points a game in 2021. She had an unusual job after the season. She became an assistant coach for the NBA Dallas Mavericks. "I loved it right away," she said. "This was what I wanted to do." Dallas coach Jason Kidd added, "She's had a big impact. ... She is knowledgeable."

Angeles finished 13-21. It was still good enough for the playoffs. The Storm swept them in the first round.

The 2011 season was like the previous one. The Sparks started 4–3, but again Parker sustained an injury. They finished the season three games out of the playoffs with a 15–19 record.

In 2012, Los Angeles drafted forward Nneka Ogwumike with the first overall choice. The team broke out of the gate 7–1 and kept going. A mid-season nine-game winning streak helped them finish 24–10. Point guard Kristi Toliver averaged more than 17 points a game. She was named as the league's Most Improved Player. Los Angeles swept the San Antonio Silver Stars in the conference semifinals. The Lynx, though, swept the Sparks in the conference finals.

GETTING TO THE THIRD TITLE

Another good start and a pair of six-game winning streaks helped Los Angeles finish 24–10 again in 2013. They split the first two games in the conference semi-finals with the Mercury. Phoenix rookie center Brittney Griner sank a short jump shot with 4.9 seconds remaining in Game 3 to give the Mercury a 78–77 series-winning victory.

Los Angeles couldn't manage any sustained winning streaks and finished 16–18 in 2014. They lost to the Mercury in the conference semifinals. Los Angeles lost the first seven games in 2015. They did manage an 11–6 record in the second half of the season and finished 14–20. They faced the Lynx in the conference semifinals. Los Angeles missed a potential game-tying basket at the buzzer in Game 1. Minnesota escaped with a 67–65 win. The Sparks won Game 2. Minnesota took the deciding Game 3.

That set the stage for the turnaround in the 2016 season. By this time, the Sparks revolved around a "Big Three" of Parker, Ogwumike, and Toliver. They opened the season with 11 wins in a row. After their first loss, the team rattled off another streak of nine wins. They finished 26–8.

The WNBA had a new playoff format. The top eight teams qualified, regardless of conference. The first two rounds were single games. Because of their record, the Sparks had byes in those rounds. They easily defeated the Chicago Sky in the first two games of the best-of-five league semifinals. Chicago won Game 3 by four points. The Sparks opened a 55–31 halftime lead in Game 4 and cruised to a 95–75 win.

Now they faced the Lynx for the WNBA title. The teams were tied 76–76 with moments left in Game 1. The Lynx focused on guarding Parker and Ogwumike. That left guard Alana Beard momentarily by herself. She took a pass and sank the winning jump shot just before the buzzer. "I don't think I've ever hit a game-winner, so it's pretty cool," Beard said. The Lynx took two of the next three. That set the stage for Ogwumike's heroics to give Los Angeles its third title. Only the Comets and the Lynx, each with four, have more.

The 2017 season was almost identical. Los Angeles had winning streaks of eight and seven games and finished 26–8 again. They swept the Mercury in the

Alana Beard

CANDACE PARKER
FORWARD/CENTER
HEIGHT: 6-FOOT-4
SPARKS SEASONS:
2008-20

OUT OF THE SHADOWS

Candace Parker grew up in the shadow of her father and older brother. Both were outstanding basketball players. Parker didn't think she could rise to their level of excellence. She played soccer instead. Her father finally convinced her to switch to basketball when she was in the eighth grade. She made rapid progress. In 2003 and 2004, Parker became the only two-time girl winner of the *USA Today* National High School Player of the Year. She helped the University of Tennessee win back-to-back national championships in 2007 and 2008. Twice she was named the National Player of the Year. She was the top overall choice in the 2008 WNBA Draft. She averaged nearly 17 points and 9 rebounds per game with the Sparks. She was a six-time All-Star. In 2021, she joined teammates Lisa Leslie and Nneka Ogwumike on The W25. It honors the league's 25 greatest players on the 25th anniversary of its founding.

LOS ANGELES SPARKS

league semifinals. They met Minnesota again for the WNBA title. Chelsea Gray's jump shot with two seconds left gave Los Angeles an 85–84 win in Game 1. But Minnesota won three of the next four to take the title.

TIME TO REGROUP

The Sparks started the 2018 season with a 9–2 record. They finished 19–15. They defeated the Lynx, 75–68, in the first round of the playoffs. But the Washington Mystics routed Los Angeles, 96–64, in the second round. With 16 points, Parker was the only Los Angeles player in double figures.

Forward Chiney Ogwumike joined her sister In Los Angeles in 2019. She averaged nearly 10 points a game. The Sparks stood just 10–8 at the halfway point. After that, a five-game winning streak immediately followed, Los Angeles closed with six wins in its final eight games. They finished 22–12. After a first-round bye in the playoffs, they defeated the Storm in the second round. Connecticut swept them in the league semifinals.

Due to the COVID-19 pandemic, the 2020 season started late. The schedule was reduced to 22 games. All were played without spectators in Bradenton, Florida. An early nine-game winning streak helped the Sparks to a final 15–7 record. Guards Brittney Sykes and Riquna Williams each averaged more than 10 points per game. After a first-round bye, the Sparks lost to Connecticut in the second round.

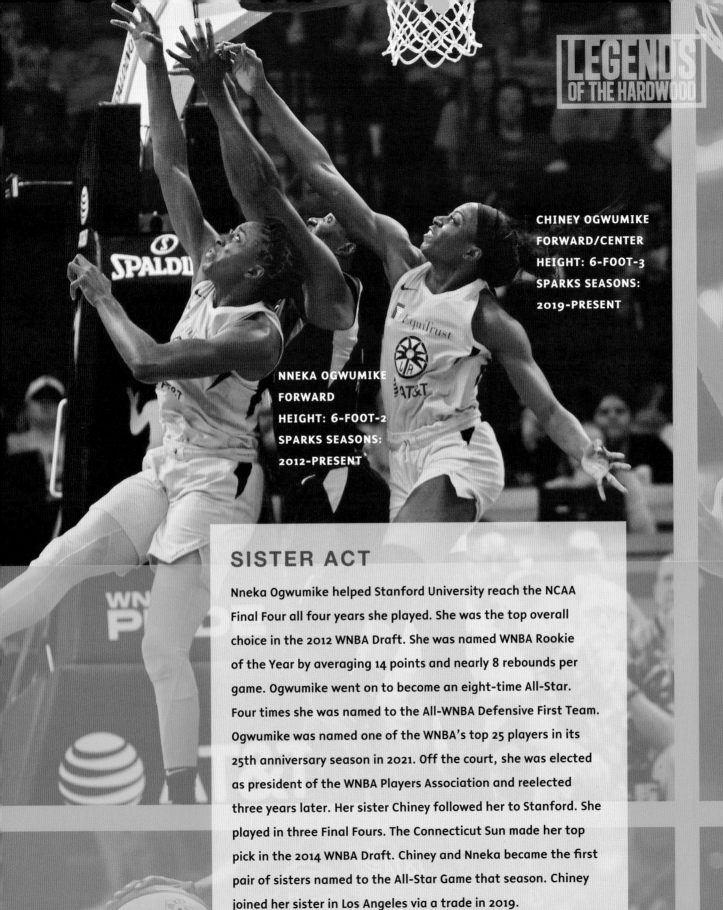

CHINEY OGWUMIKE
FORWARD/CENTER
HEIGHT: 6-FOOT-3
SPARKS SEASONS:
2019-PRESENT

NNEKA OGWUMIKE
FORWARD
HEIGHT: 6-FOOT-2
SPARKS SEASONS:
2012-PRESENT

SISTER ACT

Nneka Ogwumike helped Stanford University reach the NCAA
Final Four all four years she played. She was the top overall
choice in the 2012 WNBA Draft. She was named WNBA Rookie
of the Year by averaging 14 points and nearly 8 rebounds per
game. Ogwumike went on to become an eight-time All-Star.
Four times she was named to the All-WNBA Defensive First Team.
Ogwumike was named one of the WNBA's top 25 players in its
25th anniversary season in 2021. Off the court, she was elected
as president of the WNBA Players Association and reelected
three years later. Her sister Chiney followed her to Stanford. She
played in three Final Fours. The Connecticut Sun made her top
pick in the 2014 WNBA Draft. Chiney and Nneka became the first
pair of sisters named to the All-Star Game that season. Chiney
joined her sister in Los Angeles via a trade in 2019.

LOS ANGELES SPARKS

27

Jordin Canada

Parker returned to her hometown of Chicago to play for the Sky before the 2021 season. After starting 2021 at 5–5, Los Angeles fell below .500. They could never rise back to that level. They finished 12–20. It was the third-worst season in team history. The Sparks missed the playoffs for the first time since 2011.

To beef up the team for the 2022 season, Los Angeles signed four-time All-Star center Liz Cambage. She had set the league single-game scoring record of 53 points with the Tulsa Shock in 2018. She was happy to be with the Sparks. She had "LA" engraved on one of her teeth. "It's going to be the most wild summer the WNBA has ever seen," Cambage said in April, "and we're going to have a [championship] ring at the end of it." Unfortunately for Sparks fans, Cambage was wrong about the ring. One primary reason was that she was right about the "wild" part. It began when the team fired coach Derek Fisher 12 games into the season. It peaked with nine games remaining when Cambage quit the team. At that point, the Sparks were 12-15. That would have been good enough for the sixth seed in the playoffs. Los Angeles won just one of the next six games. Yet they were still in playoff contention. They suffered blowout losses in the final three games to finish 13–23. They missed the playoffs.

The Los Angeles Sparks have long been one of the WNBA's most exciting teams. They have also been one of the most successful. They have three championships and another 17 playoff appearances. Fans eagerly await a fourth title.

Nneka Ogwumike

INDEX